PAUL SIMON

SURPRISE

AMSCO PUBLICATIONS
part of **THE MUSIC SALES GROUP**
New York/Nashville/London/Paris/Sydney/Copenhagen/Berlin/Tokyo/Madrid

COVER PHOTOGRAPH COURTESY OF WARNER RECORDS
PIANO/VOCAL ARRANGEMENTS FOR PUBLICATION BY DAVID PEARL
PROJECT EDITOR: DAVID BRADLEY

COPYRIGHT © 2006 BY PAUL SIMON (BMI)
ALL RIGHTS RESERVED. INTERNATIONAL COPYRIGHT SECURED.

THIS BOOK PUBLISHED 2006 BY AMSCO PUBLICATIONS,
A DIVISION OF MUSIC SALES CORPORATION, NEW YORK

ALL RIGHTS RESERVED. NO PART OF THIS BOOK MAY BE
REPRODUCED IN ANY FORM OR BY ANY ELECTRONIC OR MECHANICAL MEANS,
INCLUDING INFORMATION STORAGE AND RETRIEVAL SYSTEMS,
WITHOUT PERMISSION IN WRITING FROM THE PUBLISHER.

ORDER NO. PS 11605
ISBN-10: 0.8256.3472.5
ISBN-13: 978.0.8256.3472.7

EXCLUSIVE DISTRIBUTORS:
MUSIC SALES CORPORATION
257 PARK AVENUE SOUTH, NEW YORK, NY 10010 USA
MUSIC SALES LIMITED
14-15 BERNERS STREET, LONDON W1T 3LJ ENGLAND
MUSIC SALES PTY. LIMITED
120 ROTHSCHILD STREET, ROSEBERY, SYDNEY, NSW 2018, AUSTRALIA

PRINTED IN THE UNITED STATES OF AMERICA BY
VICKS LITHOGRAPH AND PRINTING CORPORATION

HOW CAN YOU LIVE IN THE NORTHEAST?

Words and Music by Paul Simon

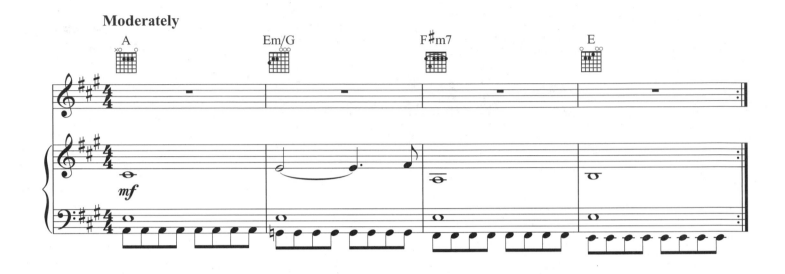

6.

I've been giv-en all__ I want-ed.

On - ly three_____ gen - er - a - tions off the boat. I have

har - vest-ed and I have plant-ed._____ I am wear-ing my fa-ther's old_____

____ coat._____

EVERYTHING ABOUT IT IS A LOVE SONG

Words and Music by Paul Simon

Driving beat

wait for the hour_____ of my res-cue.

We don't_ mean to mess things up,_ but mess them up we do._ And then it's,

"Oh, I'm sor-ry."_____

OUTRAGEOUS
Words and Music by Paul Simon and Brian Eno

Who's gon - na love you when your looks are gone?_

Tell me, who's gon - na love you when your looks are gone?_____

SURE DON'T FEEL LIKE LOVE

Words and Music by Paul Simon

gain.   I re-mem-ber once in a load-out,   down   in   Bir-ming-ham._____

Yeah,   but that did-n't feel like   love.   Sure don't   feel like,_____

G

sure don't   feel like,_____   sure don't   feel   like love._____

1.

2.

It   sure.   Don't_   feel.   Like love._____

Additional lyrics

2. A teardrop consists of electrolytes and salt.
    The chemistry of crying is not concerned with blame or fault.
    So, who's that conscience sticking on the sole of my shoe?
    Who's that conscience sticking on the sole of my shoe?
    'Cause it sure don't feel like love.

WARTIME PRAYERS

Words and Music by Paul Simon

Moderately

Prayers offered in times of peace are silent conversations. Appeals for love, or love's release. In private invocations.

BEAUTIFUL
Words and Music by Paul Simon

Moderately

1. Snow-man sit-tin' in the sun does-n't have time to waste. He had a
2. *See additional lyrics*

lit-tle bit too much fun, now his head's e-rased. Back in the house,

fam - 'ly of three: two do - in' laun - dry and one in the nurs - 'ry. We

brought a brand_ new ba - by back from Bang - la - desh, thought we'd name her Em -

- i - ly.__ She's beau - ti - ful._____

Beau - ti - ful._____ Beau - ti - ful._____

We brought a brand new ba - by back from Ko - so - vo.

That was near - ly sev - en years a - go. He cried all night.

Could not sleep. His

eyes were bright,_____ dark and__ deep._____

Beau - ti - ful.___

Beau - ti - ful._____

Beau - ti - ful._____

Beau - ti - ful._____

rit.

Additional lyrics

2. Yes sir, head's erased,
   Brain's a bowl of jelly.
   Hasn't hurt his sense of taste,
   Judging from his belly.
   But back in the house,
   Family of four now:
   Two doin' the laundry and
   Two on the kitchen floor.

   We brought a brand new baby
   Back from mainland China,
   Sailed across the China Sea.
   She's beautiful.
   Beautiful.

I DON'T BELIEVE
Words and Music by Paul Simon

soled. I lean clos - er to the fire, but I'm cold.

The earth was born in a storm.
May-be the heart is part of the mist.

The wa-ters re-ced-ed,_____ the moun-tains were

formed.
ist.

"The u - ni - verse loves_____ a dra - ma,"* you know.
May-be and may - be and may-be some more.

And

la - dies and gent-le-men this is the show.____
May-be's the ex - it that I'm look-ing for.____

I got a call from my
I got a call from my

* Observation by E.B. after 2004 presidential election

laugh-ing, not a whis-per of care. My love_____ is brush-ing her

long, chest-nut hair._____ I don't be - lieve a heart can be filled to the

brim then van - ish like mist as though life were a whim.

D.S. al Coda

Coda

shak - en._____ Acts of kind - ness, like rain in a

ANOTHER GALAXY
Words and Music by Paul Simon and Brian Eno

On the morn-ing of her wed-ding day,_____ when no one was a-wake,

ONCE UPON A TIME THERE WAS AN OCEAN

Words and Music by Paul Simon and Brian Eno

Once up-on____ a time_____ there was an o - cean. But now____ it's a moun-tain

to Coda ⊕

think-ing a - bout___ quit - tin'. And I think a - bout quit - tin' ev - 'ry

day of the week.___ When I look out my win - dow_ it's brown___ and it's bleak.___

Out - ta here.___ How'm I gon - na get out - ta here? I'm think - ing

out - ta here. When am I gon - na get out - ta here? And

gold - en thread.____ The choir sang, "Once____ Up-on A Time____ There Was An O- cean." And

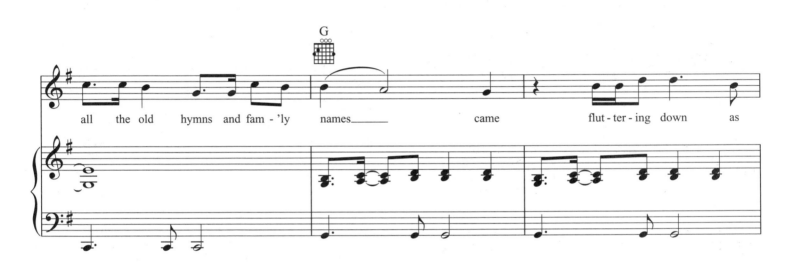

all the old hymns and fam - 'ly names_____ came flut - ter - ing down as

leaves of e - mo - tion. As noth-ing___ is diff-'rent, but ev - 'ry - thing's___ changed._

Additional lyrics

2. Found a room in the heart of the city,
   Down by the bridge.
   Hot plate and T.V. and beer in the fridge.
   But I'm easy, I'm open—that's my gift.
   I can flow with the traffic,
   I can drift with the drift.
   Home again?
   Naw, never going home again.
   Think about home again?
   I never think about home.

THAT'S ME
Words and Music by Paul Simon

65.

FATHER AND DAUGHTER
Words and Music by Paul Simon